THE LIFE
AND PRAYERS OF SAINT
BENEDICT

1

Publishing by Wyatt North Publishing, LLC. A Boutique Publishing Company.

Wyatt North Publishing, LLC
P.O. Box 120787
Boston, MA 02112

About Wyatt North Publishing

Wyatt North Publishing is a boutique publishing company that always provide high quality, perfectly formatted, Books.

All of our eBooks include a Touch-or-Click Table of Contents, allowing easy and instant access to each section.

We guarantee our Books. If you are not 100% satisfied we will do everything in our power to make you happy. Visit WyattNorth.com for more information. Please feel free to contact us with any questions or comments. We welcome your feedback by email at info@WyattNorth.com.

Foreword

St. Benedict was not interested in fame, power, or legacy. He was only interested in living the Christian life to the fullest and helping those around him to do the same. The rest is history—and the work of Providence.

St. Benedict is regarded as the Father of the Benedictine Order of both religious men and women that follow his Rule, a key principle of which is *ora et labora*—pray and work.

Today, many people wear holy medals of St. Benedict, invoking his intercession for protection against the powers of evil. Not only consecrated religious but also many lay people find inspiration in his call to balance, discipline, and prayer. Historically, St. Benedict helped bridge the early Church with the medieval period by standing on the shoulders of the fathers of the monastic tradition and bringing that tradition solidly into a new era.

Table of Contents

The Life and Saint Benedict

Introduction

St. Benedict of Nursia (480–547), the "Father of Western Monasticism," is both challenging and inspiring to us. In the midst of our busy lives, it is good for us to pause to reflect on the life of a great man of our ancient heritage who marched to the beat of a higher drummer. St. Benedict's serene trust in God, his battle with the devil and with his own tendencies, his discipline and leadership, and his life of prayer beckon us to look within and to sharpen our resolve. St. Benedict's story is also important in appreciating an institution that was central to the development of Western civilization—the monastery.

St. Benedict earnestly believed that one who is a spiritual leader for others must first conquer himself. This is precisely what St. Benedict did, and the fruits were manifold not only for his own monks but for all Europe and the Church for ages to come. He is revered for his holiness of life, for his silence, penitence, and wisdom, for his many miracles, and for his dramatic fight against demonic forces. Living at a time of great social and political upheaval in central Italy during the decline of the Roman Empire, St. Benedict helped provide peace and stability within the walls of the monasteries. He is particularly remembered for his monastic rule, appreciated for its balance, moderation, wisdom, and universality, which spread as a guide for monastic life throughout Europe for centuries and became foundational centers for its often troubled society. Largely due to the influence of his rule in equipping monasteries to play a key role in the formation and edification of Europe, St. Benedict was proclaimed co-patron of Europe by Pope Paul VI in 1964. Because of his influence on Europe, Pope Benedict XVI chose the saint for the patron of his pontificate, which was dedicated to the rebuilding of Christian Europe. St. Benedict's feast day is July 11.

St. Benedict is regarded as the Father of the Benedictine Order of both religious men and women that follow his Rule, a key principle of which is *ora et labora*—pray and work.

Today, many people wear holy medals of St. Benedict, invoking his intercession for protection against the powers of evil. Not only consecrated religious but also many lay people find inspiration in his call to balance, discipline, and prayer. Historically, St. Benedict helped bridge the early Church with the medieval period by standing on the shoulders of the fathers of the monastic tradition and bringing that tradition solidly into a new era.

St. Benedict was born in 480 in Nursia, a town in the midst of the beautiful hills, valleys, and lakes of central Italy. Sent in his adolescence to complete his classical education in Rome, the young St. Benedict was scandalized by the lax morality and wild partying of his fellow students and left to find peace as a hermit, stopping first at Enfide and then settling in a cave among the hills of Subiaco. St. Benedict later became a leader of a number of monastic communities—most famously Monte Cassino—and a writer of his influential monastic rule intended for governing that community.

Politically, his time in history was very turbulent as "barbarian" tribal armies slowly pillaged and seized key parts of the once glorious Roman

Empire, including Rome itself. Civilized people had begun losing confidence in earthly rulers. Christianity had emerged as the dominant religion, yet morals were often lax and paganism still had its adherents, especially in the countryside. Many of the barbarian conquerors had been converted to Christianity but often in a heretical Arian form that denied the full divinity of Christ, as taught to them by Arian missionaries years before their conquest.

The only source contemporary to St. Benedict that documents him is the *Dialogues* of Pope St. Gregory the Great (540–604), a man who provided strong leadership in Rome in the absence of stable secular authorities. St. Gregory, a monk himself raised to the See of Peter, wrote his *Dialogues* in the form of a dialectic conversation with his subdeacon Peter about saintly miracle workers in Italy, in effect contrasting the impotence of secular powers to the power of God. He writes of St. Benedict in the second book of his *Dialogues,* giving us a patchwork of inspirational stories from the saint's life that paint a picture for us of his holiness, miracles, exorcisms, and monastic community. St. Gregory also praises St. Benedict's Rule, which likewise gives us a picture of St. Benedict's values and lifestyle.

St. Benedict and the Monastic Tradition

While St. Benedict is indeed known as the "Father of Western Monasticism," Benedictine scholars remind us that he was not alone in his influence but emerged as a key leader within the monastic tradition for the West (see *RB 1980: The Rule of St. Benedict in Latin and English with Notes*, edited by Timothy Fry, O.S.B., to look further into the historical background on monasticism presented here). Monasticism, which entails a permanently celibate Christian life set apart from society for the pursuit of spiritual perfection, grew as a movement several centuries prior to St. Benedict. In the early days of the Church, heroic virtue was clearly seen in the sacrifice of the martyrs during the Roman persecutions. But after the Emperor Constantine not only legalized Christianity in 313 but later even granted Christians a privileged place under the law, this led to a new laxity within the Church. More believers came to the Church with insincere motives and lack of fervor. As a response, some of those that desired the full vitality of Christian life as witnessed in the martyrs set out for a separate life of prayer and fasting in the desert—a white martyrdom of death to self each day.

Finding its roots in the New Testament itself, monasticism has for its archetype St. Antony of Egypt (251–356), whom St. Benedict likely took as a model for himself. As recorded by St. Athanasius in his famous "Life of Antony," the saint personally responded to the counsel of Jesus to the Rich Young Man: "If you wish to be perfect, go, sell what you have and give to [the] poor, and you will have treasure in heaven. Then come, follow me" (Mt. 19:21 [NABRE]). Upon being struck by this passage of Scripture, St. Antony did just that, and like

Jesus in his temptation in the desert, set out alone to the desert to seek perfection and hence to battle against the forces of evil, both in their temptations and physical manifestations. During his long life in the desert, St. Antony deeply contemplated short passages of Scripture and strove to live them out perfectly.

Monastics accepted the teaching of St. Paul: "For if you live according to the flesh, you will die, but if by the spirit you put to death the deeds of the body, you will live" (Rom. 8:13 [NABRE]). They discerned a great discrepancy between our bodily tendencies and the law of God. Monastics strove to return as far as possible through prayer and self-denial to the original state of harmony from which humanity had fallen through sin and hence to experience Christ more deeply.

While St. Antony spent much of his time alone as a hermit, those later seeking this kind of life would often come together, actively practicing the communal dimension of Christ's teachings on love of neighbor. In the East, St. Pachomius (292–348) in Egypt and St. Basil (330–379) in Asia Minor established monastic communities and wrote monastic rules to govern them. In living out their communities' rules, obedience became key for monks in order to direct their fallen tendencies back to the Creator's intent and to serve the greater good of the community.

Monasticism slowly spread from the eastern part of the Roman world to the western part in which St. Benedict lived. Other monasteries were established prior to St. Benedict in the West. St. Martin of Tours (316–397), for example, had established monasteries in Gaul, and St.

Augustine (354–430) did the same in Roman North Africa; soon monasteries sprouted throughout the West. St. Benedict emerged out of the monastic tradition that came before him. But he became known as "Father of Western Monasticism" largely due to the widespread use of his rule in the West, providing organization and discipline for monasteries, bridging these traditions to medieval Europe, and paving the way for the monastery to become a bedrock of society in the midst of troubled times.

Early Life and Beginnings

Not many details are known about St. Benedict's early life, but St. Gregory's *Dialogues*—from which is derived most of what we know and which is retold below of the saint's life—provides us with some important background. He was born in Nursia, about 100 miles northeast of Rome, to noble parents. He had a sister named Scholastica—Bede tells us she was his twin—who became a nun and abbess and always maintained a close spiritual relationship with her brother. We are also told that St. Benedict had a nurse during his childhood and youth who loved him dearly and that he was provided a classical liberal education. Such an education would involve the study of grammar, logic, and rhetoric, which would prepare him to write his rule (see Carmen Butcher's *A Life of St. Benedict: Man of Blessing* for more details on the education St. Benedict would have received).

Just four years before the saint's birth in 480, Odoacer proclaimed himself king of Italy in 476 after deposing the boy emperor Romulus Augustus, placing imperial Rome under barbarian rule for the first time and foreshadowing things to come. His reign was ended in 493 by another barbarian, Theodoric the Great, who reigned for thirty years, establishing the Ostrogothic Kingdom in Italy.

St. Gregory tells us of St. Benedict that "during his boyhood he showed mature understanding, and a strength of character far beyond his years kept his heart detached from every pleasure" (quotes from the *Dialogues* of St. Gregory are translated by Odo J. Zimmermann, O.S.B. and Benedict R. Avery, O.S.B.). Perhaps this is why he was so shocked at the hedonism of his fellow students at Rome when he was sent there to complete his education. For the adolescent St. Benedict, such an environment of gluttony, drunkenness, and lust was no place for the contemplation of truth. So St. Benedict set out eastward with his nurse and stopped at the town of Enfide (later known as Affile), finding a number of holy men there.

While in Enfide, St. Benedict stayed at the Church of St. Peter, but he would not remain there for long. His nurse accidentally dropped and broke a wheat sifter she had borrowed from a neighbor. Since his nurse became quite distressed over it, the young St. Benedict knelt down and prayed, and the sifter miraculously became whole again. But St. Benedict's charity and first miracle cost him the peace he sought and made him a celebrity in the town, so much so that the sifter was even displayed for a long time in the entrance of the church there. So St. Benedict ensconced, leaving not only his prospect of a career and whole former way of life as when he left Rome but now even his beloved nurse. This time he settled down alone in the nearby wilderness of Subiaco, with its steep crags and a lake fed by a clear stream.

Solitude at Subiaco

St. Benedict found peace at Subiaco living in a cave there, and for a while he was not found by anyone who disturbed his peace. A monk named Romanus from a nearby monastery did find St. Benedict and gave him support in his new way of life by providing him with a monastic habit and regularly sharing bread with him from his own allotment. St. Benedict knew he could trust Romanus, who kept his presence there a secret, sneaking out through the untamed wilderness to bring bread and lowering it by a rope down to his cave. Romanus' kindness, however, provided the occasion for the first demonic manifestation recorded in St. Benedict's life. Once while Romanus was lowering the bread, a demon is said to have thrown a stone and shattered the bell attached to it which let St. Benedict know when to fetch the bread.

But the demons had only begun their assault on the saint. Later a demon came in the form of a blackbird fluttering about the saint's face. He banished it with the sign of the cross. But after the blackbird flew off, the demon continued its assault with an almost irresistibly strong temptation of the flesh, which St. Benedict overcame by throwing his naked body onto a thorn bush. Though badly bruised and bloodied, the saint had won a key victory in mastery over his passions such that he was never again seriously tempted to lust.

Soon St. Benedict's hiding place would be found, and it was indeed the Lord's plan since he was preparing the saint for spiritual leadership. First God revealed St. Benedict's cave to a nearby priest by way of a vision, prompting the priest to bring St. Benedict some food on Easter

Sunday. Then some shepherds stumbled across St. Benedict's hiding place and experienced an interior conversion under his influence. News of him spread around the area and many were drawn to him because of his wisdom and virtue. St. Gregory tells us that after St. Benedict's victory over his passions, he was then prepared for spiritual leadership—although it would not at all be easy.

The abbot of the monastery at Vicovaro died, and the monks were in need of a replacement. They sought out St. Benedict because of his fame, but the saint warned them that he would be strict and that his leadership would clash with their lax lifestyle. However, the monks persisted, and St. Benedict finally agreed to go to them. But as time went on, the monks became displeased with the discipline that he brought to the monastery, preferring to do as they liked as before rather than to do battle with their passions and sinful tendencies. Several of the monks even went so far as to poison St. Benedict's drink given to him at dinner. But when the saintly abbot said the blessing, making the sign of the cross, the glass shattered, and their plot was uncovered. He said, "May Almighty God have mercy on you!" And then he left those wicked men and returned to the solitude of Subiaco, realizing they would not be converted by either his leadership or example. But soon other more sincere spiritual seekers would flock to Subiaco, and some would seek to live a monastic life under him there.

Miracles at Subiaco

St. Benedict actually built 12 monasteries around Subiaco, each with a superior and 12 monks. He also served as abbot over these monasteries, governing with special wisdom and power from God. He worked many miracles which are strongly reminiscent of those in Scripture, such that St. Gregory's interlocutor, Peter, said he must have the "spirit of all the just." St. Gregory corrected him that it was not by the saints of old that St. Benedict performed his miracles but by the Holy Spirit, who likewise filled those holy men. The miracles are a sign of his being filled with the Spirit of God and are like a seal of approval on his way of life.

Once there was a monk in one of his monasteries who would always sneak off during times of silent prayer to do anything else. His superior could not get through to him, so he sent the monk to St. Benedict to admonish him. But nothing worked, and the monk went back to his old ways. Later St. Benedict saw a little boy with a sinister appearance tugging on the monk's garment during prayer and pulling him out. Realizing the monk's strange behavior was the work of a demon, St. Benedict and other monks prayed for two days, and then when the monk went out again during prayer, St. Benedict struck him with a rod afterwards, casting the demon away. The monk never had that trouble with silent prayer again.

In addition to giving him power against the devil, the Lord also gave St. Benedict miracles to supply the needs of the community. He was perhaps not the greatest of architects, but his prayers even supplied what he was lacking in that. After St. Benedict had three of his monasteries at Subiaco built on the top of a cliff with a beautiful view, the monks went to him concerned that they might have to rebuild the monasteries elsewhere because of one important problem: The water they needed had to be carried from the base of the mountain all the way up to the top of the steep cliff each day. The saint, however, was not perturbed and assured them that everything would be all right. He went to the mountaintop to pray, and placed three stones where he had prayed. Then he told the monks to dig where they found the three stones. When they followed his instructions, a spring miraculously bubbled up, like the water that Moses brought forth out of the rock in the desert. This stream permanently supplied their needs so that the monks' energies could be spent on better things.

Once while clearing out a garden on the side of the lake, one of the monks was using a sickle when the blade flew off the handle and landed in the middle of the water, quickly sinking to the bottom. The monk became very upset and anxious and confessed his fault to one of his fellow monks. St. Gregory tells us that the monk who lost the sickle blade was a Goth and that he was a sincere and simple man. Medieval studies scholar Carmen Butcher, in her book *A Life of St. Benedict*, suggests that as a Goth—a member of the race of the occupying forces—he was perhaps a former soldier of theirs, used to harsh punishment for simple mistakes. Also, as a monk, he would have been taught to respect the tools they worked with because with them they did the work of God. Seeing him in such anguish over this mishap, the other monk called over St. Benedict, who came down and took the empty handle and placed it in the water. The sickle blade was drawn from the bed of the lake up to the surface and back onto the handle. Then the abbot returned the miraculously restored tool to the monk and comforted him saying, "Continue with your work now. There is no need to be upset."

Many of St. Benedict's miracles echoed ones recorded in Scripture, as with the following miracle. St. Benedict was entrusted by a number of Roman families with bringing up their boys in the monastery and preparing them for life as monks. He was quite fond of two brothers—Marus and his younger brother Placid—who St. Gregory often points out as accompanying him in his special prayers and a number of his miracles. One day while Brother Placid was still very young and unable to swim, he fell in the stream while fetching water and was carried off into the middle of the lake. St. Benedict was immediately told by God of the boy's plight. So, he quickly summoned his brother Marus, commanded him to go and rescue Brother Placid in the middle of the lake, gave him his blessing, and sent him off to the task. But as Brother Marus raced towards Brother Placid, he never jumped into the water or swam to him but rather ran straight to him at full speed, pulling him out and bringing him back to the shore.

Brother Marus had been given the grace through St. Benedict's prayers to walk on water like the Apostle Peter, having faith in his superior's command. He did not even realize what he was doing and attributed what had happened solely to God's grace through St. Benedict's prayers. Brother Placid also said later that he had felt St. Benedict's cloak embracing him and bringing him safely home.

Despite his miracles and exorcisms, not everyone was fond of St. Benedict. As Jesus said, "If the world hates you, realize that it hated me first" (Jn. 15:18 [NABRE]). A nearby priest named Florentinus became very envious of St. Benedict because the people flocked to the abbot for spiritual guidance and inspiration rather than to him. Furthermore, while envying the saint's virtue, the priest had no desire to follow his same path to virtue. Florentinus went so far as to send St. Benedict a poisoned loaf, ironically making the semblance of a customary token of Christian fellowship (see p. 75 in Butcher's *A Life of St. Benedict*).

The abbot knew it was poisoned but thanked the priest nonetheless. Like the prophet Elisha, St. Benedict spoke to a raven and gave it instructions: It was to dispose of the poisoned loaf in a deserted area. At first the raven would not do it, but the saint commanded it again, and it obeyed. After some time, Florentinus saw that the abbot was alive and well, so he plotted spiritual ruin on St. Benedict's monks. He tempted them by sending seven naked girls to frolic about in their courtyard, instructing them to stay there a long time so the monks would be swayed to lust.

Seeing that his adversary would stop at nothing and that the whole affair was potentially becoming quite destructive to the community, St. Benedict resolved that he himself would leave since the priest's envy was directed only against him. Leaving his first monasteries in the hands of worthy superiors, this closure would open up a new chapter for St. Benedict at a new monastery he would build at Monte Cassino.

But before he reached his destination, Brother Marus ran up to him on the way and happily informed him that God had struck down Florentinus in judgment—that the walls of the room Florentinus was in crashed down upon him and killed him.

St. Benedict, however, was saddened and chastised Brother Marus for being so glad at such somber news.

Battling the Devil at Monte Cassino

Monte Cassino is about 80 miles southeast of Subiaco, the site of a shrine to Apollo on the side of a tall mountain and also of an abandoned citadel that would make a good place for a monastery. Likely arriving there in 529, St. Benedict first had to clear out the place and dedicate it to God. He tore down the altar to Apollo, felled the sacred trees, transformed the temple into a chapel, and converted the local adherents of the cult of Apollo by his preaching. St. Gregory tells us that this greatly upset the devil, who appeared to St. Benedict as a flame-breathing figure. Even the monks could hear this devil's invective, to which the saint would not respond. Further angered, the devil taunted St. Benedict: "Maledict, not Benedict!"—which literally means "cursed, not blessed." He continued, "What do you want with me? Why are you tormenting me like this?" But St. Benedict knew his adversary.

So the devil tried to thwart the building process and harass the monks as much as possible. While the monks were constructing the abbey, they came upon a rock that they could not lift even though it should have been a fairly simple task. More monks came to help raise it, exerting all their strength, but it would not budge. The monks asked for St. Benedict to come, and with his prayers and the sign of the cross, the rock was suddenly freed and became very easy to move. But St. Benedict still sensed a presence there and commanded the monks to dig at that spot—and sure enough, they found a bronze idol. And the trouble didn't stop there.

The monks carried the idol into the kitchen until they had time to deal with it. Suddenly flames appeared, exploding out of the idol and consuming the kitchen, and the monks could not put out the flames. Then St. Benedict arrived in his typical complete serenity. To him, there were no flames—only a demon, which he soon chased away with his prayers. Sure enough, the flames disappeared, and the kitchen was left unscathed.

But the devil would not be cast off so easily. While St. Benedict was praying in his room, the devil came and taunted the saint, smirking that he would be stopping by to pay the monks a visit later that day. The abbot sent warning to the builders, but it was too late—just then the wall they were constructing crashed down, crushing a young monk and killing him. When the monks reported the tragedy to the saint, he instructed them to bring the body up to him and leave him alone to pray. Within an hour, the same monk emerged from St. Benedict's room, his life restored and his broken bones perfectly healed. With much rejoicing, the monks finished constructing the wall together with their restored brother.

St. Benedict's Gift of Prophecy

With St. Benedict as abbot, no one could get away with anything because he was given supernatural knowledge of events that concerned him and those around him. He did not have this knowledge of his own power, but it was given to him by God at certain times for the spiritual edification of others.

Since the monks lived a life intentionally set apart from society, there were specific rules for traveling in the outside world that made it clear that they were only wayfarers there. One of these rules was that they were not to eat or drink along the way. But one time they did, and when they returned, they asked St. Benedict for his blessing. He knew they had eaten along the way and asked them about it. They denied it but became very nervous as St. Benedict recalled to them exactly what they had eaten, how much they had drunk, and where. After they admitted it and apologized, the saint forgave them and warned them not to do it again.

There is another story much like this. One of the monk's brothers from back home would often make a pilgrimage to the monastery, committing to fast along the way. But once one of his companions passing the same direction tried three times to get him to eat. The first and second time the man refused, explaining that he was fasting, but the third time he was swayed and took the food. When he arrived at the monastery and asked the abbot's blessing, the saint chastised him and recounted the whole affair to him. The man was very penitent.

Not even kings could get away with anything with St. Benedict. King Totila, the Ostrogoth ruler, had heard reports of St. Benedict's prophetic abilities and decided to see for himself. He sent word to the monastery that he intended to pay the abbot a visit, and St. Benedict sent back that he was welcome, as all were. So the king decided to try to trick St. Benedict to see what powers he really had. He clothed his minister, Riggo, with the royal attire and gave him the royal entourage to see if the abbot would uncover their game. St. Benedict sat near the entrance to the monastery, watching the entourage approaching. Before they even halted, he called out, "Son, lay aside the robes that you are wearing. Lay them aside. They do not belong to you." Riggo and the entourage fell to their knees before the saint and then retreated back to their master to tell him what had happened—that they were truly dealing with a holy man.

So King Totila himself resolved to come pay respect to the holy man, and he prostrated himself before him in fear from a good ways off. The abbot bid him twice to rise and finally went over and helped him up. Then the saint chastised King Totila: "You are the cause of many evils. You have caused many in the past. Put an end now to your wickedness." He also prophesied: "You will enter Rome and cross the sea. You have nine years more to rule, and in the tenth year you will die." King Totila had been a ruthless warrior, fighting by any means against the forces of Emperor Justinian of Roman Byzantium to regain the Ostrogothic Kingdom in Italy and the city of Rome that his predecessor Theodoric the Great had once ruled over. St. Benedict's prophecies did come true. King Totila conquered Rome in 549.

Historians note that King Totila did indeed march through the region near Monte Cassino in 542—the likely year of the king's meeting with St. Benedict—and one of the most certain dates we have for the events of St. Benedict's life (see footnote on p. 37 of *Life and Miracles of St. Benedict (Book Two of the Dialogues* translated by Zimmermann and Avery). King Totila did in fact die in battle ten years later in 552 at Taginae. Also, even the king's biographer, Procopius, notes an ethical improvement in Totila after his meeting with St. Benedict (see p. 103 of Butcher's *A Life of St. Benedict*). However, the days of Ostrogothic occupation in Italy were numbered after King Totila's death.

St. Benedict's foreknowledge also helped him to give good counsel, and his prayers helped to free people from the grasp of the devil. A man was brought to St. Benedict, who had been tormented by an evil spirit. This man was in a clerical state but not a priest or deacon. He had already visited the shrines of the martyrs, but St. Gregory tells us that the martyrs did not heal the man so that God's work could be seen through St. Benedict. The demon was indeed cast out by St. Benedict's prayers, but the saint warned the man not to present himself for ordination or the demon would return. For a long time the man followed St. Benedict's counsel but grew ambitious when he saw younger men being ordained, so he finally accepted ordination. But just as the saint had warned him, the demon returned to torment him, and he never escaped from it.

One day a monk named Theoprobus, who was close to St. Benedict, came upon the abbot weeping in his room. He was weeping without ceasing, so Theoprobus finally asked what was wrong. St. Benedict said that it had been revealed to him that the abbey of Monte Cassino would be destroyed by barbarians and that the monks would escape only with their lives. Sure enough, the Lombard Duke Zotto destroyed the monastery in the late 6th century, several decades after the saint's death (see footnote on p. 44 of *The Life and Miracles of St. Benedict* translated by Zimmermann and Avery). It was eventually rebuilt in 720. St. Gregory, who by his time was already recording the destruction as a historical fact, compared St. Benedict's misfortune with that of St. Paul, who was shipwrecked and lost everything except his life and the lives of those aboard.

Not only was St. Benedict given knowledge of events that happened far away or in the future, but he was given knowledge of people's hidden thoughts as well. Monks rotated certain duties, and among those was bearing a lamp for the abbot while he ate. One particular monk, who came from a noble family, entertained prideful thoughts while performing this duty, silently asking himself who this man was that he should be holding a lamp for him while he ate.

St. Benedict said to him, "Brother, sign your heart with the sign of the Cross. What are you saying? Sign your heart!" St. Benedict then had a different monk hold the lamp while the first one sat silently.

The monk did not know for certain which fault the abbot was referring to until he asked him afterward. St. Benedict told him that it was for his silent prideful thought that the abbot had been given to hear.

Miracles at Monte Cassino

St. Benedict trusted in God for all his needs, and when famine hit the region and his monastery was out of supplies, there was no difference. Historians do indeed document a great famine of 537–538 in the region of Campania, in which Monte Cassino is located (see footnote on p. 47 of *Life and Miracles of St. Benedict* translated by Zimmermann and Avery).

Eventually the monks' supplies dwindled such that the bakers were only able to come up with five loaves of bread to be shared by the large community and then ran out entirely. Many of the monks became very disconcerted that they would all soon starve. But St. Benedict admonished them, "Why are you so depressed at the lack of bread? What if today there is only a little? Tomorrow you will have more than you need." Sure enough, a large pile with many sacks of flour was found at the monastery's gate the next day. The monks never did find out where these supplies came from—whether God had moved a benefactor to drop off the precious load or whether he produced it purely by a miracle. Either way, God supplied their needs just at the time they needed it—no sooner and no later.

As St. Benedict grew older, God even enabled the saint's spirit on at least one occasion to travel where his body did not. St. Benedict sent off a group of monks to found a new monastery on the estate of a pious benefactor who had invited them there. The land was at Terracina, a coastal town about 30 miles to the southwest. Before giving the monks his blessing, St. Benedict told them he would come on a certain day to direct them on where and how to build the new monastery.

The morning of that given day, the superior and his assistant shared with each other that they had each had the same dream in their sleep that night of St. Benedict giving them the plans for the new monastery. But still not understanding that it was the abbot himself who had truly been given to come to them in their dreams, they were still watching and waiting for his physical arrival. They even became quite disappointed when he never came, so they set off on foot for Monte Cassino to find out what had delayed him. But when they asked him, St. Benedict replied, "What do you mean? Did I not come as I promised? Did I not appear to both of you in a dream as you slept and indicate where each building was to stand? Go back and build as you were directed in the vision."

The vision they had received was indeed so clear and consistent that they were able to go back and build the monastery in just the way that St. Benedict desired.

It was a rule that any monks leaving on a journey had to ask for the abbot's blessing and his permission—and even more so to leave for good. But once a new and young monk became homesick and simply ran off from the monastery to go back home, neglecting his duties and the rule. Upon reaching home, the monk immediately fell dead. Not only did he die, but after he was buried, his body would not stay in the grave but rose to the top, simply lying on top of the ground. His parents were naturally quite distressed—and even more so when after they buried him a second time and the same thing happened.

So, the parents came to the abbot to ask him to forgive the monk and to enable their son to rest in peace. There was a pious tradition during that time to bury the faithful with a consecrated Host on their chest (see footnote on p. 55 of *Life and Miracles of St. Benedict* translated by Zimmermann and Avery). So St. Benedict gave the parents a consecrated Host and instructed them to bury their son again with the Blessed Sacrament upon his chest. Only then was the monk able to be at rest in his grave. St. Gregory tells us, "Not even the earth would retain the young monk's body until he had been reconciled with blessed Benedict."

There was another monk who was thinking about leaving the monastery as well, although he did discuss it with St. Benedict. The abbot could not persuade the monk by talking to stay the course that God had prepared for him, so he eventually gave him permission to go his own way. But just as the monk was stepping out, a devil appeared ahead of him on the path as a ravenous dragon ready to devour him— its prey. The monk shrunk away in terror, calling out for help since he was still in shouting distance of the monastery. The monks rushed out to help him, but the devil was invisible to them. So the monk happily returned to life at the monastery, realizing that his urge to leave was from the promptings of the tempter.

One day a faithful layman, who was burdened with unbearable debt, approached St. Benedict for help since his creditors were threatening him more and more and he had no way to repay them. The man owed 12 gold pieces—a whole year's wages. St. Benedict felt sympathy for the man but did not have any money to help him with, so he told him to come back in two days. With the saint's prayers, 13 gold pieces appeared in the monastery on top of a chest of grain. So when the poor man came back, St. Benedict was able to give not only enough gold to pay off his debt but even an extra piece to help supply his daily needs while he struggled to support himself.

During the great famine, a subdeacon was in dire need of oil and came to the monastery begging for a little oil. Even though there were only a few drops of oil left among their own supplies, St. Benedict resolved to give it to him and instructed the monk in charge of the supplies to do so. But when the subdeacon came to the monk to get the oil, the monk refused to give it over because then there would not be enough for the monastery. So the subdeacon went away empty-handed. St. Benedict asked the monk if he had obeyed his order to give the supplies to the cleric in need. He replied that he did not, because of their own shortage. The abbot commanded him to throw the glass jar with the few precious drops of oil out the open window to fall down a rocky cliff. This time the dismayed monk obeyed, but the jar was miraculously protected from the rocks, and the oil was saved.

St. Benedict called the monks together and admonished them that they must give to the needy when called on—and especially when ordered by their superior—and trust God with the rest. Then they knelt down to pray. While they prayed, a large empty jug in the room that used to be filled with oil slowly began to be filled with oil again. As St. Benedict and his monks prayed, the oil kept rising until it spilled over the top of the jug and onto the floor. At that, St. Benedict realized it was time to stop praying, and the oil likewise stopped rising.

During the occupation by the Ostrogoths, one of King Totila's captains, Zalla, plagued the region and oppressed the people as suited his own whims. Zalla was an Arian heretic in addition to being a man of greed and violence, so he often mistreated and took advantage of orthodox Catholics that were under his power—even killing many clerics. One day Zalla tried to extort a poor Catholic farmer for money. The man told him he had no money, but Zalla beat and tortured him until he at last screamed out that Abbot Benedict had his money. With that, the torture stopped, but Zalla bound the poor man's hands, tied the rope to his horse, mounted the animal, and forced the man to lead the way to Abbot Benedict. When they arrived at Monte Cassino and came upon St. Benedict, Zalla sat high on his steed and roared at the abbot to hand over the money the man had given him.

St. Benedict looked up serenely and then set his eyes on the poor man whose hands were bound to the horse. Immediately, the tight and heavy ropes fell to the ground. Zalla became very much afraid of the abbot's mysterious power and got down trembling and bowed to him, pleading for his prayers. St. Benedict invited Zalla in for dinner and admonished him to turn from his evil ways. The poor farmer was never bothered by Zalla again.

Another farmer came to St. Benedict with his plight—his young son had tragically died. He went to the monastery in search of the abbot, who was just coming back from working out in the fields with the other monks. As the abbot approached, the man called out to him, "Give me back my son! Give me back my son!"

St. Benedict replied, "But I have not taken your son from you, have I?" The man explained that his son had died, and that since he had heard so much of St. Benedict's miracles, he believed that surely his prayers could raise his son back to life. St. Benedict was much saddened and perplexed; he said to his monks, "Stand back, brethren! Stand back! Such a miracle is beyond our power."

The distraught farmer kept pleading. St. Benedict had worked so many other miracles. Surely God would hear him with this too. At last, the abbot agreed to pray, and they led him to the little body laid before the entrance of the monastery. St. Benedict knelt over the boy, raised up his hands in prayer, and then cried out, "O Lord, do not consider my sins but the faith of this man who is asking to see his son alive again, and restore to this body the soul you have taken from it."

The lifeless body began once again to stir as the boy's soul reentered it, and St. Benedict helped the child to his feet. The father's faith had been rewarded, and he was overjoyed to return home with his beloved son alive and well.

Last Days and Heavenly Longings

St. Benedict was blessed with a twin who was a sister to him not only biologically but also spiritually—St. Scholastica. Like her brother, she had lived a long and godly life from the start. She, too, pursued Christian perfection by way of a monastic life, consecrated in virginity from a young age. St. Benedict and St. Scholastica were accustomed to their yearly visit at a house just outside Monte Cassino in which they would always discuss God and the soul. They always enjoyed their visits in moderation, but on one certain visit, St. Scholastica particularly enjoyed their company.

Even after hours of enlightening spiritual conversation during the day and into the evening, she asked her brother to stay with her through the night to contemplate the things of God. Ever the strict and disciplined abbot, St. Benedict refused because, according to the rule, all monks had to be home by a certain time—and the abbot was no exception but instead had to set an example for the rest. St. Scholastica folded her hands in prayer and suddenly a violent thunderstorm erupted with a torrential downpour that made the climb back to the monastery unsafe. St. Benedict exclaimed, "God forgive you, sister! What have you done?"

 St. Scholastica replied, "When I appealed to you, you would not listen to me. So I turned to my God, and he heard my prayer. Leave now if you can. Leave me here and go back to your monastery."

Since the storm prevented him from leaving, St. Benedict and St. Scholastica spent the whole night discussing the wonders of God and the glories of heaven and were very edified and refreshed by it. The storm subsided by daybreak, and the twins bid each other goodbye and went their own ways. But only three days later, St. Scholastica went to her final reward. St. Benedict was 'given to see his sister's soul leave her body and rise to heaven in the form of a dove, and he rejoiced that she had at last come to the heavenly glory that she had so much desired while on earth. St. Scholastica was buried at Monte Cassino in a tomb that they would one day share.

St. Benedict had another friend who would also visit him periodically to speak of the heavenly things—a deacon named Servanus, who was also an abbot in the same region. St. Gregory writes of them, "In speaking of their hopes and longings they were able to taste in advance the heavenly food that was not yet fully theirs to enjoy." One dark night during one of Servanus' visits, St. Benedict went up to his room to pray.

As he looked out his window, a great light was cast down from heaven that lit up the landscape as bright as day, and out of the heavenly stream of light, St. Benedict was given to see the whole world in a single instant, in a way reminiscent of how the blessed in heaven are able see all things in God. Meanwhile angels were flying up to heaven, carrying a globe of fire that contained a soul that St. Benedict could tell was that of Germanus, bishop of Capua—a town about 75 miles southeast of Monte Cassino. St. Benedict wanted very much for his friend Servanus to share this vision, so he called out to him several times, even though he was getting ready for bed on the floor beneath.

Finally, Servanus heard him and ran up the steps just in time to share in the beauty of this vision before it was taken away. St. Benedict sent for news of Bishop Germanus, and the messenger returned with word that the bishop of Capua had indeed parted this life on that very night.

St. Benedict wanted very much to share in the heavenly glory that he knew his sister and the bishop of Capua now enjoyed. Secretly, he foretold his own death to certain monks, and then six days before he died, the abbot ordered for his grave to be opened. After giving this strange order, the saint developed a fever and became increasingly ill. When he knew his appointed time had come, he instructed his monks to carry him into the chapel. There he received holy Communion—his bread for the journey—before having his brothers support him as he stood up with arms outstretched to heaven in prayer. In this way, he passed on, his body resting upon the shoulders of his spiritual sons and thoughts set on what is above.

That day two of his monks in different locations were given a confirmation of their abbot's destiny. They were each given to see a brilliant heavenly staircase that rose eastwards—towards God's rising Son—with an angel at its base who announced to them that the abbot had passed this way into God's kingdom. But even while enjoying the glories of heaven, St. Benedict did not forget those on earth. St. Gregory tells us that St. Benedict's miracles did not cease with his death but that he continued to look down on God's people from heaven with his fatherly solicitude.

The Rule of St. Benedict and His Legacy

While those who knew St. Benedict remembered him for his holiness of life and his many miracles and prophecies, history remembers him especially for his monastic rule (the commentary in *RB 1980* edited by Timothy Fry, O.S.B., is quite helpful in further understanding St. Benedict's Rule and its impact on history). His rule was a piece of writing that he drew up during his days as abbot of Monte Cassino that was intended to govern the way of life at the monastery in order to make it a school of Christian perfection and to guide the monks in monastic wisdom that could otherwise take a lifetime to possess. St. Benedict envisioned the monastery as a place where brothers dwell as one in a balanced, discipled, and rigorous pursuit of Christ's teachings and where the abbot was to be obeyed and revered as spiritual father, accountable to God for the salvation and spiritual progress of each of his sons.

For the wisdom of the rule, St. Benedict drew from the monastic tradition, from Scripture, and from years of personal experience in the monastery and before that as a hermit. He did not see himself as an author of an important literary work but as a father setting down principles and guidelines for his sons. He did not even sign his name to the rule. Some scholars have found that much of the content of his rule is actually not original but was drawn from a much longer text called the "Rule of the Master," written by another monastic leader whose identity is unknown to history and who likewise drew heavily from St. John Cassian. However, St. Benedict's rule in comparison with the "Rule of the Master" is much shorter and more concise, is more moderate and less severe, and envisions God more as a loving Father than as a wrathful Judge.

For St. Benedict, a monastic rule is a guide to living out Scripture, so Scripture permeates nearly every page. The Abbot of Monte Cassino begins his rule with words reminiscent of the Wisdom literature from the Old Testament: "Listen carefully, my son, to the master's instructions, and attend to them with the ear of your heart. This is advice from a father who loves you; welcome it, and faithfully put it into practice. The labor of obedience will bring you back to him from whom you had drifted through the sloth of disobedience" (translation as edited by Timothy Fry, O.S.B., in *RB 1980*).

The word "abbot" means father, and this figure plays strongly in the rule since a man of prayer, virtue, love, discipline, and impartiality is required to make this "school for the Lord's service" work as it should. He must not use his position for power but is accountable to God for all his actions and decisions regarding his brothers. Humility and obedience are important for the monk, especially on account of man's disordered tendencies. Humility is required to recognize those tendencies and obedience to set them aright.

The rule promotes a balanced life of prayer and work. As was customary at that time, the Liturgy of the Hours, with its psalms and readings chanted by the monks, was called the "Work of God." It provided the rhythm for life and physical work at the monastery. From Vigils at 4 a.m. to Compline at 7 p.m., the Work of God, interspersed with set activities such as physical labor, eating together, meditating or studying, and gathering consecrated each of these activities to God (see a schedule for a Benedictine monk's day on p. 158-159 of Butcher's *A Life of St. Benedict*).

As seen in the story of St. Benedict as retold by St. Gregory, the rule set guidelines for monks who were traveling. They were required to return the same day and avoid eating along the way unless instructed to do so by the abbot, and they were to complete the Work of God as they would at the monastery. There were also many other guidelines governing situations common in monastic life so that the monks would conduct themselves in such a way that furthered the good of the whole community and the pursuit of spiritual perfection. At the end of his rule, St. Benedict tells us that the rule can only point the way of the beginnings of the spiritual life; the rest must be learned through meditating on and constantly living out Scripture and the teachings of the Church Fathers.

Besides the wisdom within its pages, the Rule of St. Benedict was more ideal than other monastic rules for being widely circulated and implemented. It is more general than many of the other rules in existence whose guidelines tended to be specific to only particular communities; its relatively short length made it easier for monks to copy in the days before the printing press; and it accommodated for Roman liturgical practices, which later became universalized in the West.

St. Benedict's Rule was spread throughout Europe and became the most widely implemented monastic rule for both men and women religious. When Monte Cassino was destroyed by the Lombards in the late 6th century, the monks who fled were able to take with them at least one thing with them besides the clothes on their back—a manuscript of the Rule, which governed Monte Cassino again when it was rebuilt in 720. Irish, English, and Gallic monastics visiting Rome copied the Rule of St. Benedict and implemented and circulated it in their home countries by the 8th century.

When Charlemagne sought to unite diverse parts of Europe under his Holy Roman Empire, he tried to bring together his subjects through religious unity in the Roman forms of worship. To this end, he enforced the Roman liturgy throughout the empire and promoted the Rule of St. Benedict for the monasteries, though never completing the full unity of the monasteries under this rule. The abbey of Cluny was founded in 910 and adopted the Rule of St. Benedict. This abbey was destined to establish a vast and socially powerful network of abbeys and priories throughout all of Europe, spreading the Rule of St. Benedict throughout the continent.

As the centuries went on, Cluny's social power eventually yielded to spiritual laxity and required reformers like St. Bernard of Clairvaux to return to the strict observance of St. Benedict's Rule. This pattern of laxity and reform would become a trend in the world of Benedictine monasteries over the coming centuries. In the 13th century, new forms of religious life suited to the special challenges of the age emerged through the initiative of St. Francis of Assisi (the Franciscans) and St. Dominic de Guzman (the Dominicans) and in the 16th century through St. Ignatius of Loyola (the Jesuits), but Benedictine monasticism—following the Rule of St. Benedict—retained its special place in the life of the Church. Following the Protestant Reformation, the Rule of St. Benedict continued on in monasteries even until this day in the Anglican and Lutheran traditions.

While some contemporary monasteries follow the Rule of St. Benedict as literally as possible, many approach it as a guide of wisdom given the differences in culture from our day to that of St. Benedict. Many lay people also draw inspiration from the rule, likewise approaching it as wisdom literature. One famous recent return to a stricter observance of the rule was at the abbey of Solemnes in France beginning in the latter part of the 19th century. The abbey is especially known for producing some of the most influential reform-minded liturgical scholars of the 20th century. Some other monasteries continue a strict observance today.

In 1964 Pope Paul VI proclaimed St. Benedict Patron of Europe. Paul VI praised the work of St. Benedict and the monks and nuns who followed his rule throughout the centuries for their contribution to the building of Europe with "the cross, the book, and the plow."

He writes in his Apostolic Letter *Pacis Nuntius*: "With the cross; that is, with the law of Christ, he lent consistency and growth to the ordering of public and private life…. With the book, then, i.e., with culture, the same St. Benedict...saved the classical tradition of the ancients at a time when the humanistic patrimony was being lost, by transmitting it intact to its descendants, and by restoring the cult of knowledge. Lastly, it was with the plow, i.e., with the cultivation of the fields and with other similar initiatives, that he succeeded in transforming wastelands gone wild into fertile fields and gracious gardens; and by uniting prayer with manual labor, according to his famous motto 'ora et labora,' he ennobled and elevated human work."

St. Benedict was not interested in fame, power, or legacy. He was only interested in living the Christian life to the fullest and helping those around him to do the same. The rest is history—and the work of Providence.

Prayers by Saint Benedict

Prayer for the Gifts to Seek God and Live in Him

Father, in your goodness grant me the intellect to comprehend you, the perception to discern you, and the reason to appreciate you. In your kindness endow me with the diligence to look for you, the wisdom to discover you, and the spirit to apprehend you. In your graciousness bestow on me a heart to contemplate you, ears to hear you, eyes to see you, and a tongue to speak of you. In your mercy confer on me a conversation pleasing to you, the patience to wait for you, and the perseverance to long for you. Grant me a perfect end - your holy presence. Amen.

Saint Benedict on Prayer

Prayer ought to be short and pure, unless it be prolonged by the inspiration of Divine grace. - Saint Benedict

"In the first place, beg of Him by most earnest prayer, that He perfect whatever good thou dost begin, in order that He who hath been pleased to count us in the number of His children, need never be grieved at our evil deeds. For we ought at all times so to serve Him with the good things which He hath given us, that He may not, like an angry father, disinherit his children, nor, like a dread lord, enraged at our evil deeds, hand us over to everlasting punishment as most wicked servants, who would not follow Him to glory."

Girded with a faith, and the performance of good works, let us follow in Christ's path by the guidance of the Gospel; then we shall deserve to see him "who has called us into his kingdom." If we wish to attain a dwelling place in his kingdom, we shall not reach it unless we hasten there by our good deeds. Just as there exists an evil fervor, a bitter spirit, which divides us from God and leads us to hell, so there is a good fervor which sets us apart from evil inclinations and leads us toward God and eternal life. No one should follow what he considers to be good for himself, but rather what seems good for another. Let them put Christ before all else; and may he lead us all to everlasting life. - from the Rule of Saint Benedict

Prayers to Saint Benedict

Prayer I

Admirable Saint and Doctor of Humility, you practiced what you taught, assiduously praying for God's glory and lovingly fulfilling all work for God and the benefit of all human beings. You know the many physical dangers that surround us today, often caused or occasioned by human inventions. Guard us against poisoning of the body as well as of mind and soul, and thus be truly a "Blessed" one for us. Amen.

Prayer II

Glorious Saint Benedict, sublime model of virtue, pure vessel of God's grace! Behold me humbly kneeling at your feet. I implore you in your loving kindness to pray for me before the throne of God. To you I have recourse in the dangers that daily surround me. Shield me against my selfishness and my indifference to God and to my neighbor. Inspire me to imitate you in all things. May your blessing be with me always, so that I may see and serve Christ in others and owrk for His kingdom.

Graciously obtain for me from God those favors and graces which I need so much in the trials, miseries and afflictions of life. Your heart was always full of love, compassion and mercy toward those who were afflicted or troubled in any way. You never dismissed without consolation and assistance anyone who had recourse to you. I therefore invoke your powerful intercession, confident in the hope that you will hear my prayers and obtain for me the special grace and favor I earnestly implore. {mention your petition}

Help me, great Saint Benedict, to live and die as a faithful child of God, to run in the sweetness of His loving will, and to attain the eternal happiness of heaven. Amen.

Prayer III

Gracious and Holy Father,

give us the wisdom to discover You,
the intelligence to understand You,
the diligence to seek after You,
the patience to wait for You,
eyes to behold You,
a heart to meditate upon You,
and a life to proclaim You,
through the power of the Spirit of Jesus, our Lord.

Prayer IV

Father, in Your goodness

grant me the intellect to comprehend You,
the perception to discern You,
and the reason to appreciate You.
In Your kindness
endow me with the diligence to look for You,
the wisdom to discover You,
and the spirit to apprehend You.
In Your graciousness
bestow on me a heart to contemplate You,
ears to hear You,
eyes to see You,
and a tongue to speak of You.
In Your mercy confer on me
a conversation pleasing to You,
the patience to wait for You,
and the perseverance to long for You.
Grant me a perfect end,
Your holy presence.

Amen.

33722719R00040

Made in the USA
Middletown, DE
24 July 2016